Church of Irela

025038

Franklin Watts
96 Leonard Street
London EC2A 4RH

Franklin Watts Australia
14 Mars Road
Lane Cove
NWS 2066

Franklin Watts Inc.
387 Park Avenue South
New York, N.Y. 10016

UK ISBN: UK Edition 0 86313 917 5
US ISBN: 0-531-10849-X
Library of Congress No:

Editor: Ruth Thomson
Design: K & Co

The Publisher and Photographer
would like to thank
Messinger Tools of Guildford
for their kind help and assistance.

Typeset in England
by Lineage, Watford
Printed in Italy by
G. Canale S.p.A., Turin

Publisher's note:
Many of the tools shown in this
book can be dangerous. Children
should never be allowed to use them
without adult supervision.

Ways to....
CUT it!

Henry Pluckrose

Photography by Chris Fairclough

FRANKLIN WATTS
London • New York • Sydney • Toronto

These are all tools used for cutting. They have many different uses.

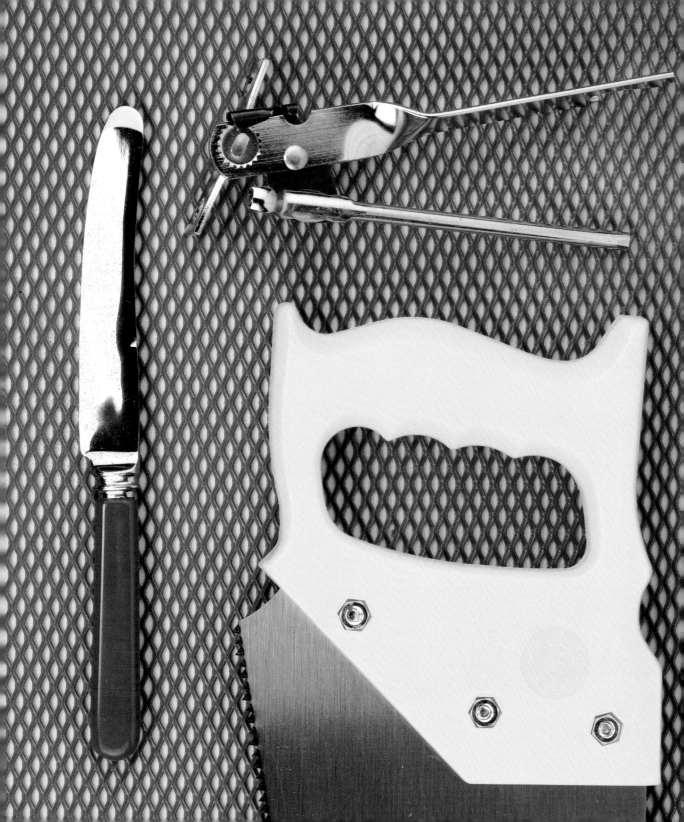

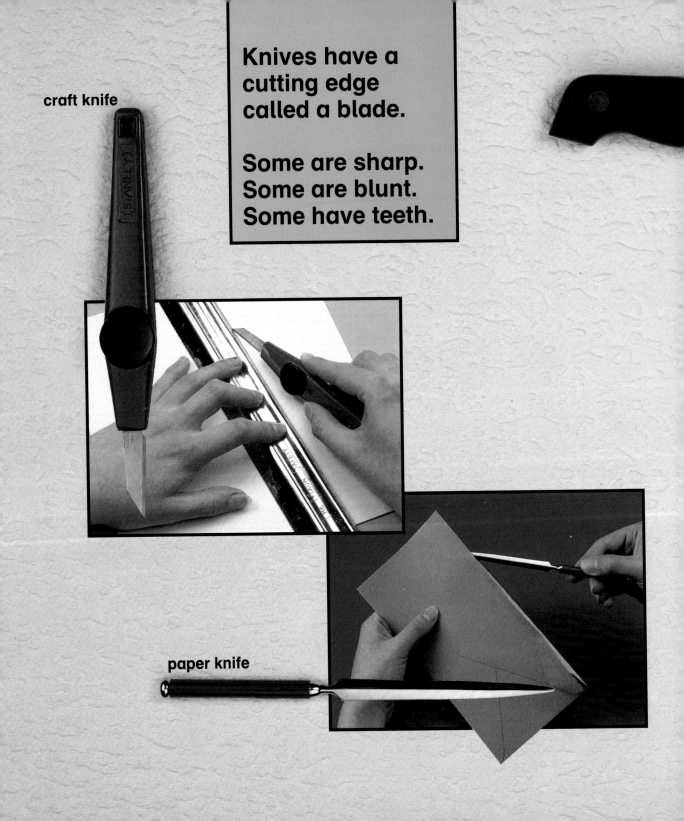

craft knife

Knives have a
cutting edge
called a blade.

Some are sharp.
Some are blunt.
Some have teeth.

paper knife

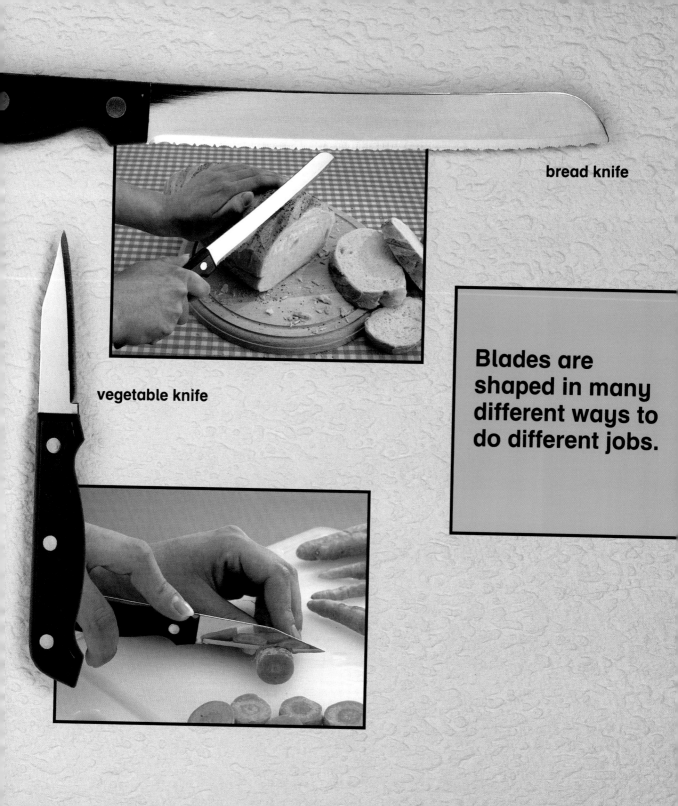

bread knife

vegetable knife

Blades are shaped in many different ways to do different jobs.

A blade is always harder than the material it cuts.

We could not use a wooden knife to carve wood...

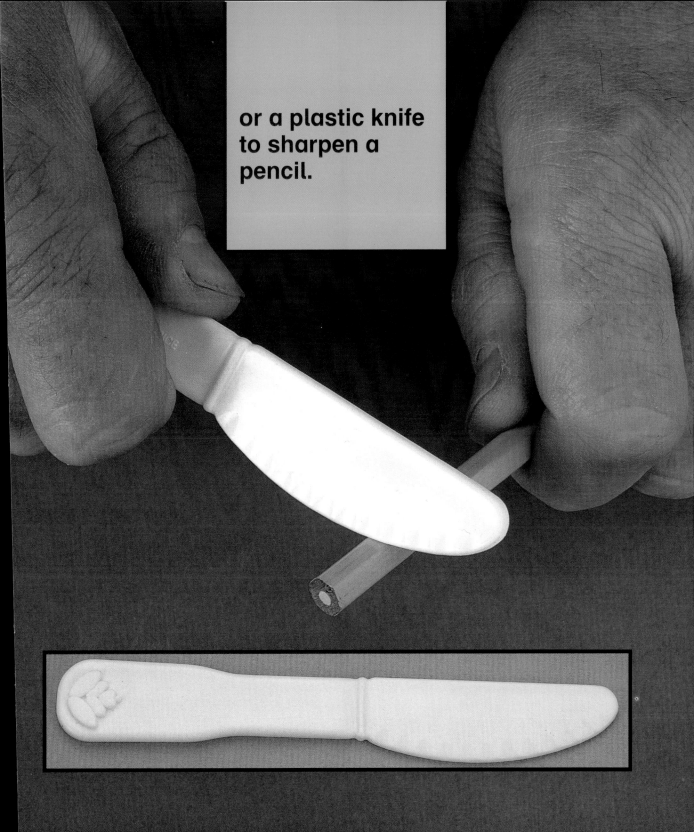

or a plastic knife to sharpen a pencil.

vegetable knife   steak knife   penknife

Compare the shapes of these blades.

They are well-suited for the jobs they do.

meat knife   table knife   cheese knife

Some blades have a toothed edge. The large teeth of this saw tear through wood.

This saw cuts
through metal.
The blade has
small hard teeth.

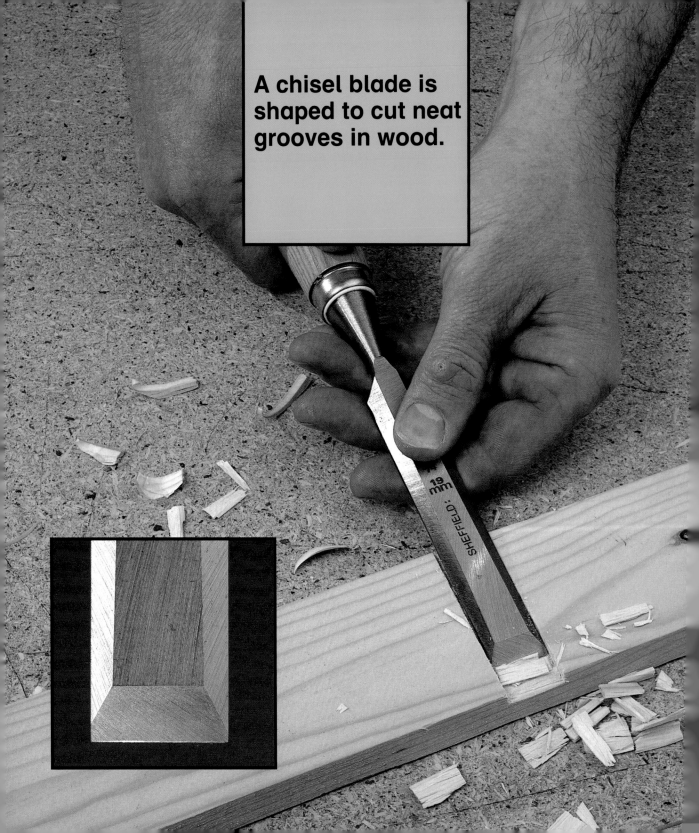

A chisel blade is shaped to cut neat grooves in wood.

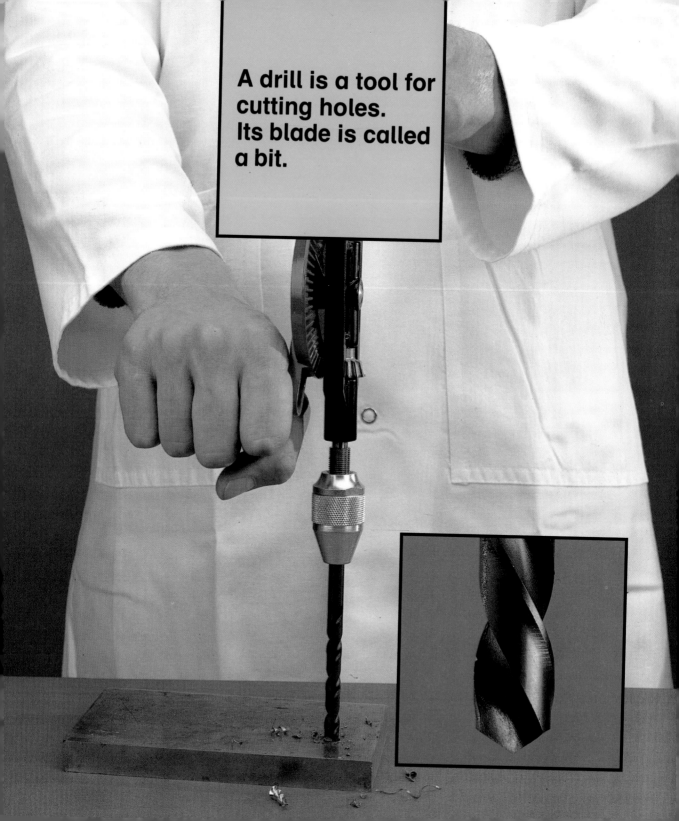

**A drill is a tool for cutting holes.
Its blade is called a bit.**

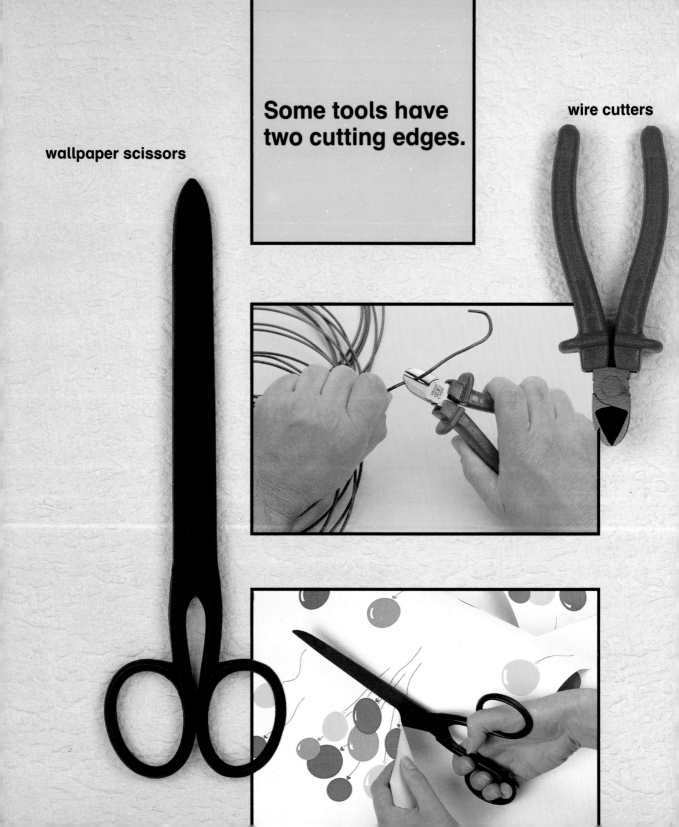

wallpaper scissors

Some tools have two cutting edges.

wire cutters

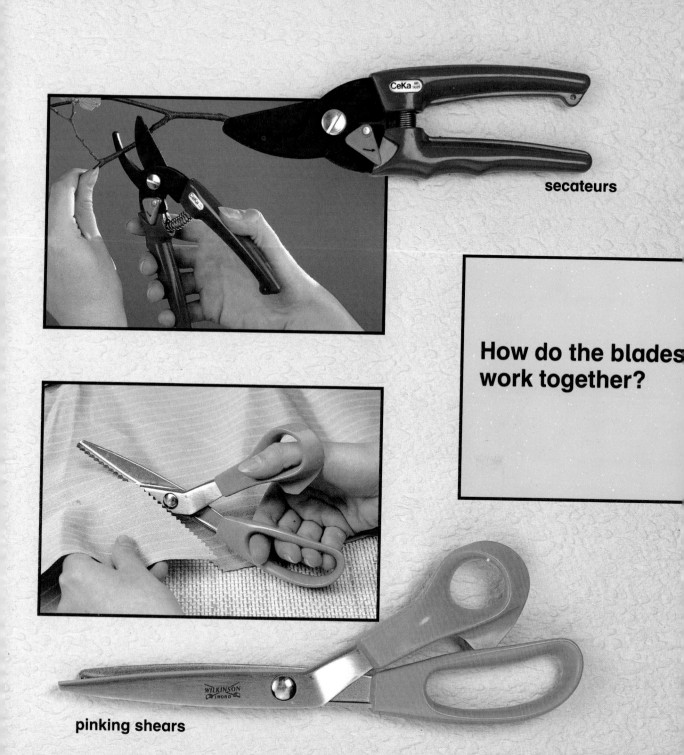

secateurs

How do the blades work together?

pinking shears

garden shears

nail clippers

sewing scissors

dressmaker's scissors

hair scissors

children's scissors

tin cutters

tree pruners

These are more tools with two cutting edges.

Watch how the blades move together to cut.

To cut anything,
the cutting edge of
a tool must move.
A knife cannot cut
butter by itself!

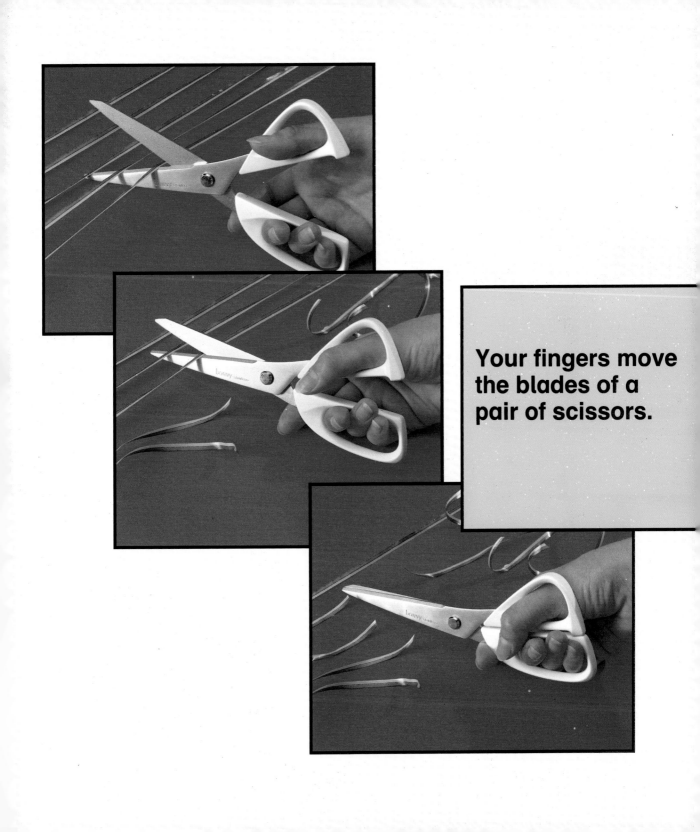

Your fingers move the blades of a pair of scissors.

circular saw

These tools are powered by electricity.

masonry drill bit

chain saw

What other sorts
of energy can be
used to power
tools?

16"
40 CM Black

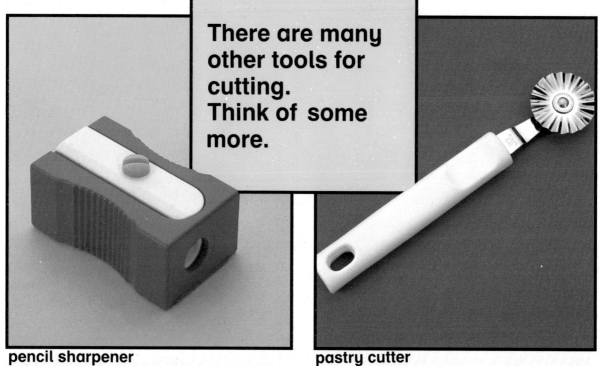

There are many other tools for cutting. Think of some more.

pencil sharpener

pastry cutter

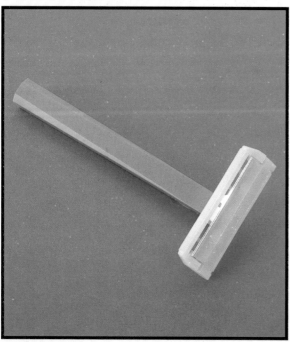

safety razor

lawn mower

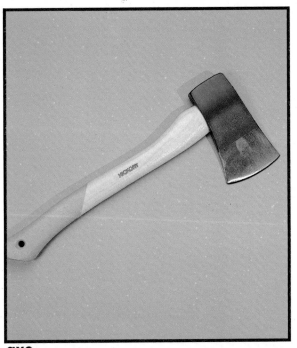

axe

stone chisel

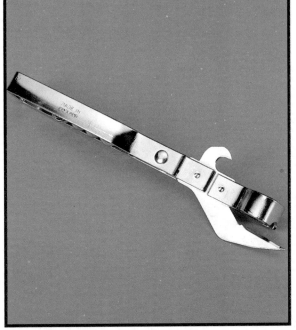

can opener

spade

Some things to do

● Take a piece of paper.
Fold it in half.
Tear along the fold.

Take a second piece of paper. Without folding the paper first, can you tear it neatly in half?

Look at the edges of the sheets you have torn. Are they uneven or do they have a clean, sharp edge?

Take a third piece of paper. Cut it in half using scissors. Which of the three methods gives the cleanest cut? Which leaves the roughest cut? How do the folds help you to tear paper neatly?

● Your sharp front teeth cut through the food you eat. Can you bite into a slice of bread without using your lower jaw?

Which part of your face moves when you bite and chew your food?

● Find an unplanted piece of ground (the edge of a flower bed will do very well).

Try to make a hole in the ground, using the following tools:
● a thick piece of wood
● a piece of wood with one end sharpened to a point
● a piece of cardboard
● a plastic plate
● a metal trowel
● a sharp pointed stone

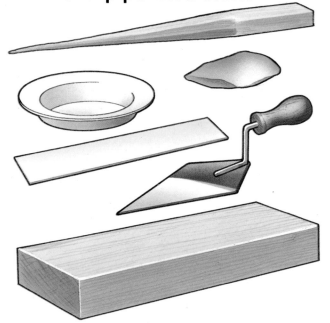

Which of these tools are easy to use for digging? Which cut into the ground easily? Which do not cut at all?

Try making a simple paper cut.
● Fold a square of paper
(25cm x 25cm) into quarters.

Using scissors, cut little
pieces from each edge of
your folded paper square.

Open the paper to see the
pattern you have cut in it.

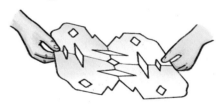

See what happens if you cut
all of the edge away.
   Can you make a pattern
by tearing the edge of a
folded sheet?

Words about cutting

axe	raze
carve	saw
chop	scythe
clip	sever
cut	shave
fell	shear
gash	shorten
hew	slice
lop	smooth
mow	snip
nip	split
plane	tear
plow	trim
prune	

Cutting tools

axe	plane
can opener	pliers
chisel	plow
chopper	pruning shears
clippers	razor
cutters	saw
drill	scissors
hatchet	sharpener
knife	shears
knives	space
mower	wire cutters
penknife	

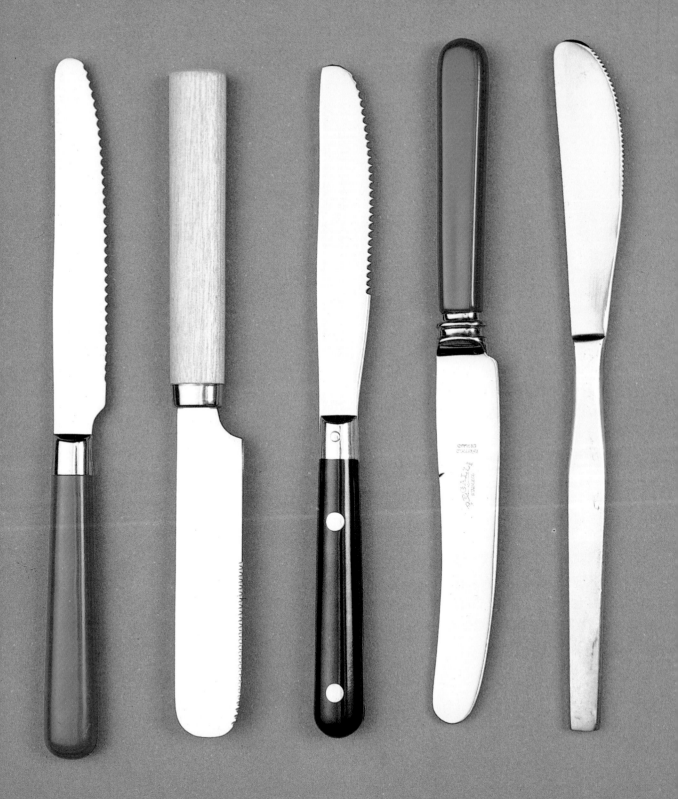